GREG PRINCE ON GAY LDS HISTORY, PRIESTHOOD, LEADERSHIP, AND WORD OF WISDOM

Copyright © 2017

Gospel Tangents

All Rights Reserved

Except for book reviews, no content may be reproduced without written permission.

Table of Contents

Introduction – page 3

Part 1 – History of LDS Policy Toward Gays – page 4

Part 2 – "There is Nothing in LDS Policy that Justifies Whacking Infants" – page 15

Part 3 – The 4 LDS Leadership Vacuums – What Happened? – page 20

Part 4 – Ailing Church Leaders – "Not Ideal Governance" – page 27

Part 5 – Early LDS Priesthood: Similar to Ancient Christianity? – page 37

Part 6 – Naturalistic Explanation for Word of Wisdom? – page 47

Part 7 – When did LDS Start Ordaining Youth? – page 57

Epilogue – page 62

Additional Resources – page 63

Introduction

Gospel Tangents needs your support. Please consider donating to our website, https://GospelTangents.com in any amount. We will use your donation, and the information from these podcasts to produce professional Mormon History Documentaries and other resources such as this.

Greg Prince delivered the Sterling McMurrin Lecture in September 2017. Rick Bennett of *Gospel Tangents* sat down with Greg to discuss his upcoming book detailing the history of how the LDS Church has dealt with gay members, as well as several other topics the First Vision, the Word of Wisdom, women giving blessings, dealing with ailing church leaders, succession, and when young men began to be ordained to the Aaronic Priesthood. It's a fascinating discussion. Greg answers these and many other questions.

(Note this conversation was recorded on September 27, 2017 in Salt Lake City, Utah. I will use GT for Gospel Tangents to indicate when I am talking to Greg. The interview has been lightly edited to remove verbal miscues.)

History of LDS Policy Toward Gays

The Interview

GT: Welcome to Gospel Tangents. I'm excited to have Greg Prince here. Greg is one of the best historians that I know of in all of LDS scholarship. Greg can you tell us why you're here in Salt Lake City today?

Greg: I am here to deliver the *Sterling McMurrin Lecture*[1] this evening at the Salt Lake Public Library. This is sponsored by the Tanner Center of Humanities at the University of Utah, and the topic that I will be addressing will be the biology of homosexuality, and how that relates to LDS Church policy.

GT: Ok, so I was thinking this was going to be more of a science thing. So there is science involved.

Greg: There is science.

GT: I just actually interviewed Dr. Ugo Perego.[2] I don't know if you know him. We talked a lot about DNA and the Book of Mormon,[3] and Biblical Literalism,[4] and that sort of thing. That's what I was thinking you were going to be talking about. This will be interesting. I know that earlier this week you spoke with Doug Fabrizio on *Radio West*,[5] and that

---

[1] Watch video at https://www.youtube.com/watch?v=gssnz1WZ3dU&t

[2] Interview at https://gospeltangents.com/2017/08/23/dna-101-dr-ugo-perego/

[3] Interview at https://gospeltangents.com/2017/09/16/doesnt-dna-match-book-mormon-part-1/

[4] Interview at https://wp.me/p8l6gx-iz

[5] Interview at http://radiowest.kuer.org/post/history-mormons-and-homosexuality

was a fascinating interview. I don't know. Would you like to talk a little bit about—just kind of give us a little preview, although this is going to be aired long after today, but tell us a little bit about—I believe you're writing a new book. Is that right?

Greg: Yes.

GT: Tell us a little bit about that book.

Greg: The book looks at the relationship between the LDS Church and LGBT issues and people for the past half century. I started in the late 1960s because that's when it first became a recognizable issue in the church. The word "homosexuality" or any of its variants did not appear in the General Handbook of Instructions until 1968, and then it appeared once without any explanation.

GT: That just kind of boggles my mind. Why do you think it didn't appear until the '60s?

Greg: Why didn't it appear in American society? It was 1968. The following year was the Stonewall Riot in New York City.[6] That wasn't the initial foray into gay rights in the American consciousness, but it catapulted it forward. Really the LDS Church was pretty much in sync with the rest of the country in not having pulled LGBT issues out of the closet.

GT: Ok, I believe, I want to say Gary Bergera wrote a history on one of the church patriarchs if I remember right that had an issue with homosexuality which was before the '60s. Are you familiar with that?

Greg: Yes.

GT: Can you tell us a little bit about that?

____

[6] Basic information can be found at
https://en.wikipedia.org/wiki/Stonewall_riots

Greg: It's still a matter of controversy, and I've spoken with his son, not Gary's son but the patriarch's son who takes issue with it and says, "No that wasn't the case." But nonetheless it was in the 1940s, and the patriarch, whose name sounds like another church leader, Joseph Fielding Smith, was quietly released from his duties as a patriarch, and spent the rest of his life living in Hawaii. But the issue was never a public issue. He was officially released "for health reasons."

{break}

GT: We were talking a little bit about the church patriarch. Was his name Joseph Fielding Smith?

Greg: Yes.

GT: It was, but it was a different person.

Greg: A cousin.

GT: A cousin, ok. So the official reason was for health reasons, but...

Greg interrupts: That remained the official reason. To this day, family members so no, it wasn't the case and so I'll leave it at that.

GT: Ok. So you're not going to second-guess what other reason it was?

Greg: No. I have no information that would allow me to do that.

GT: Ok. As far as Gary's work, how do you...?

Greg interrupts: Gary will have to stand behind his work.

GT: Alright, cool. It does seem that there may have been something going on. There may have been as early as the [19]40s but there was no formal church discipline for gay members, or do you know how that works?

Greg: There was nothing in the General Handbook of Instructions, which is the LDS equivalent of Catholic canon law, so if there had been any disciplinary action taken in earlier years, it would have been on an ad-hoc basis and I have no information that would tell me if and when and how often that might have been done.

But in terms of homosexuality being an issue that was finally openly presented within the church, it didn't happen until the late 1960s. Yes there were occasional, but very rare instances where a church leader might mention it in private or even in a public address, but it never climbed up the hierarchical ladder to make it into the handbook.

GT: Ok. So you're that it was pretty ad hoc then, but it probably was pretty common if somebody was gay that they were excommunicated.

Greg: What was more common in those years was if you were gay you stayed in the closet, whether it was as a Mormon or it was as a member of American society, not LDS. The downside for coming out was so extreme that very few people would have taken that initiative. That's as true for Mormonism as it was for the rest of American society.

In the 1950s with the Red Scare, homosexuality and communism often got bundled by the people who were doing the baiting, so that drove it even further underground. There were purges during the Eisenhower administration within the State Department and other government agencies, not just of communists but of gays. So why would anybody voluntarily come out in an atmosphere like that?

GT: But there were some people that were exposed because other people found out?

Greg: Sure. Look at the consequences.

GT: Ok. Can you give us a brief history from within the church? I noticed on the *Radio West* interview, one of the things you said was, there's been some fits and starts and some progress, some regression. The church doesn't seem to be following a steady path as far as treatment of gay members.

Greg: Until the presidency of Spencer Kimball, even though it was in the handbook, you didn't hear much about it. Now that interim was only 5 years between 1968 and when President Kimball became president in 1973. But in that period and for more than the decade prior to that, Spencer Kimball had as part of his portfolio as a member of the Quorum of Twelve dealing with issues of homosexuality.

So he was the one who had to review details of the cases and make recommendations as to what type of punitive action might be taken, or whether there might be restoration of blessings in the case of somebody who might have been excommunicated. So it was a continual part of his administrative diet to deal with these issues, and I think it probably worked to polarize him. Plus there was a statement that President McKay made to him where President McKay said homosexuality is a graver sin than heterosexual intercourse. Basically saying that being homosexual was a more grievous sin that committing fornication or adultery.

GT: Even if you didn't act on it, that was still worse than actually committing fornication.

Greg interrupts: When President Kimball became the church president, then that became really the standard. If you were gay, celibate or otherwise, that was grounds for excommunication.

GT: Even if you didn't act on it.

Greg: Yes, and it extended particularly broadly down at BYU where BYU Security would stake out gay bars on Salt Lake City, take down license plate numbers, and then the Honor Code Office would bring these students in and say, "Either you tell us who the other gays are on campus or we will expel you and have you excommunicated."

GT: That doesn't seem very nice.

Greg: No, and this was all for being gay. It didn't matter if you were celibate. That was certainly a low point. Eventually they moved to a slightly better position, saying, "No it's not that you're gay. It's that you're acting on your sexuality," which is essentially where we are now.

Some would say that's not much progress. At least it's a measurable change from where we used to be in the Kimball years. If you look at church policy, there have been some advances that are real advances. I think the most dramatic and maybe the most important is that a gay man or a lesbian woman can serve a full-time proselytizing mission with honor being openly gay as long as he or she remains celibate.

GT: Do you know when that change happened?

Greg: I don't recall that there was ever a written
announcement of it. I have not seen it documented, but
it's been I think at least a decade since that change
happened.

GT: Ok, so that's one of the good things.

Greg: That's one of the good things. We have had a
more compassionate general attitude towards LGBT
people in the church, of trying to appeal to parents and
other family members and fellow church members, not to
be antagonistic, not to throw the kid out of the house
which too often happened in the past and still happens
too much.

But we've also had some regression. Certainly Prop 8
marked a political low point for the church where their
role in passing Prop 8 in California was so significant that
in the minds of many people, it became known as the
Mormon Proposition. [7] Then in reaction to that, there was
a gradual realization within the state of Utah that there
needed to be some fence-mending done. In [2015][8] the
[Utah] Legislature with a big public push from the church
(otherwise it couldn't have happened), passed Senate Bill
296 which forbade by law discrimination against LGBT
people in areas of employment and housing. It was a big
step forward because Utah still is the only state whose
legislature and gubernatorial chair are occupied by
Republicans that has passed that kind of legislation.

GT: Oh really?

---

[7] Proposition 8 was a ballot initiative in November 2008 in California over the
legalization of gay marriage in the state. The LDS Church led an organized
campaign against legalization of gay marriage. Citizens in California voted
against legalization of gay marriage, but the decision was overruled in a 2013
U.S. Supreme Court decision.
[8] Greg misspoke. He said 1995 but the year was 2015.

Greg: But then later that year, the Church came out with "the Policy" and so it was another low point. We just seem to be in this cycle of a step forward and a step back, and the LGBT population in particular, since they are the one who are most affected by these things is wondering, are we really moving forward, or are we just kind of being batted back and forth?

GT: What do you think the answer is to that?

Greg: I don't know yet.

GT: I know that November Policy was hard for a lot of people. Why do you think that the policy came out in the first place?

Greg: Oh I know why it came out because I talked to a couple of the Brethren who very clearly said it was a response to the Supreme Court decision in June of that year. In March of that year you had SB 296. That was a high water mark. That was good news.

GT: That was the stop discrimination in housing and employment.

Greg: Yes. Then three months later you had *Obergefell vs. Hodges*, the decision by the U.S. Supreme Court that legalized gay marriage throughout the country. That was another high water mark for the LGBT community, but then in November of that same year you had the announcement out of nowhere of "the Policy."

Now what were the details beyond that? I don't have any firsthand knowledge of, but I do have good, reliable knowledge that the policy represented the Church's response to the Supreme Court decision. Now was it an essential response? Look at it and make up your own mind on it. You come down on various parts of that decision.

GT: Yeah let's talk a little bit about that. I actually spoke with Paul Reeve a few months ago. It was back in February. One of the questions that I asked him, you know we have the Second Article of Faith that says "Men will be punished for their own sins and not for Adam's transgression." A lot of Mormons, and I would estimate a majority of Mormons would say that basically we're punished for our own sins and not for anybody else's.

Some people say that really applies to Adam. We're not punished for Adam's sins. Yes you can be punished for someone else's sins. Let's ask you. Where do you fit on that spectrum?

Greg: Within two weeks of the announcement of the policy, I was invited by lunch with the president of Wesley Theological Seminary in D.C. It's the largest Methodist seminary in the country. Subsequent to that, as in May of this year, I was elected to membership on the board of governors of Wesley Seminary, so I have a very close relationship with him.

The president who I've known for years said, "Am I missing something here? I thought I had a reasonable understanding of LDS theology." His understanding included having been invited here to meet with the First Presidency, take the tour of BYU. He's done some homework and he's fairly knowledgeable about Mormonism and he's quite sympathetic towards it, but he said, "What it is in your theology that justifies beating up infants?"

I said, "David, there is nothing that justifies that?"

I think it's the going after the kids, but particularly the infants that has been so distasteful both to church members and to the outsiders. But I think that the damage that was done by Prop 8 was mostly external. It was an explosion.

GT: So when you're talking about beating up infants, you're talking about the idea that we won't bless children of gay parents.

Greg: Yes, the ritual of blessing in the Mormon Church, as with christening in other Christian traditions is the formal acknowledgement by the community of believers that your child exists. Your child has a name, and it's accepted by the community. We have denied that to same-sex couples, so in essence we are saying, "Your child doesn't exist."

GT: It goes beyond just infants but baptism and ordination and things like that.

Greg: It does, but the non-member standpoint, at least the president of the seminary and others I have spoken with, the thing that astounds them and troubles them the most is that we are punishing infants.

GT: That's interesting.

Greg: Now I said just a minute ago that Prop 8 was an explosion. I think the primary downside of that was primarily outside of the church. Yes it did cause dissension and it caused a lot of hurt inside the church but for the most part it was the world outside the church that just shook its head and said, "Look what the Mormons did."

With the policy was an implosion. The force was directed inward and you had tens of thousands of church members who took the rather drastic step of resigning their membership. We have no idea how many additional tens of thousands just said quietly, "That's enough. I'm out," and then walked away without going through the steps of formally resigning their membership. That didn't happen with Prop 8.

GT: I've talked to some of my friends that no longer attend. Some of them have taken their names off, some of them haven't. Do you think these mass resignations and falling into inactivity have had an impact on church leaders? Have they noticed?

Greg: They have not acknowledged publicly that they have noticed, and in fact we have had pronouncements from General Conference talks saying, "We're fine. There is no such thing as a faith crisis."

On a public level, they have not said anything that I am aware of that says, "Hey Houston, we've got a problem."

Now, what might be going on behind closed doors there, I don't know. But if the losses continue at the pace that they seem to be going since November of 2015, there's probably going to be a time pretty soon when somebody's going to be saying, "Houston we do have a problem."

GT: Do you think this was a calculated decision that yes, we might lose some members but it will level out and we'll be fine?

Greg: The way it was sprung on the church and even sprung on the quorum, members of the Quorum of Twelve said they first knew about this two days before it leaked to the public. I don't know how much calculation there was behind it. There certainly did not go through the normal process of being discussed, being vetted by the quorum and perhaps by other bodies or individuals. It was just dropped on them as a done deal without any real discussion. This is what's going to happen.

"There is Nothing in LDS Theology that Justifies Whacking Infants"

Introduction

We're continuing our conversation with Dr. Greg Prince. In our next conversation we'll ask about theological justifications of the ban. What does Greg Prince think about these justifications? We'll also ask about the common questions: will the LDS Church be forced to marry gay members in the LDS Temples? What does Greg Prince think about that? We'll talk a little bit about the history of marriage in the LDS Church for heterosexual couples, and I think Greg has an interesting point right at the outset that you may find interesting. Check out our conversation.....

The Interview

Greg: Up until 1960s within the United States you could have a civil wedding ceremony and go to the temple the next day to be sealed.

GT: Until the '60s.

Greg: Yeah, late '60s.

GT: Wow.

Greg: And then somebody got a bee in his bonnet and said, "No that degrades the sacred nature of the temple! We're going to say you can't go in for a year!" Now at the same time they said that, they were already dealing with the reality that in foreign countries, and we didn't have many foreign temples then so it wasn't that big of deal. We had the Swiss, the British, and the New Zealand temples, but nonetheless there they were. In those countries, the government does not recognize a religious ceremony.

So if you want to be married, you have to go to an official of the government, the equivalent of a justice of the peace or a court judge, and have the wedding ceremony performed. In most countries, I think most countries in the world that still is the case today. So in those countries, the church has no choice.

I suppose they could say, get married and then a year later let's get you in the temple to be sealed. In most countries they say, "You're married today, you go to the temple tomorrow." But they're still holding out in the U.S. Go figure. It's not because of any scripture. It's because in some discussion at some point somebody said, "We need to emphasize this, and so the way we're going to do it is you're going to have to wait a year."

GT: This brings it all the way back to what we started talking about at the beginning; the whole issue with the November policy was because of the gay policy, "the Policy."

Greg: The Policy was a reaction to the Supreme Court decision.

GT: Right. I know some people, and I'd love to have you comment on this, have said, "The government is going to force gay marriages in LDS temples. Number one, do you see that happening, and do you think that's a rationale that the brethren think is going to happen?

Greg: Can you think of a single instance that the government has said to a Roman Catholic priest, "You must perform the wedding of a Roman Catholic who has been divorced?"

16

GT: I can't.

Greg: Can you think of a single instance where a Jewish rabbi has been compelled by the government to perform a marriage of a Jew to a gentile?

GT: No.

Greg: Can you give me a single instance where an evangelical pastor has been compelled to perform an interracial marriage?

GT chuckles: No, but I'm hearing this as a justification for why we have "the Policy." So you're telling me that's a bad justification.

Greg: I'm telling you it's an empty justification. It's scare talk. It has no basis in reality. If you can find me one example from any of those other three categories, then we'll talk. Can you give me one example of the government compelling the church to allow somebody who does not hold a valid recommend to enter the temple for any purpose? No. See where we're going on this?

GT: So that's a bad argument.

Greg: It's not just a bad argument, it's a bankrupt argument. There's no basis in reality of making that argument.

GT: So why have this then?

Greg: Why have what?

GT: Why have this policy?

Greg: Good question. If you find out the answer, let me know. I'll give you my phone number.

GT chuckles: Now one other thing that we did talk about, I don't know that we fully answered that.

Greg: Well we're not going to totally answer anything!

GT chuckles: It's about the children. We don't want the children to be conflicted if they have gay parents. What do you think of that?

Greg: I think it's bogus. Why would a same-sex couple want their child to be blessed or baptized if their intention was to turn it away from the church?

GT: That's a great question.

Greg: The very fact that they want that ordinance performed says they're buying into this. They want to be part of that church community and they want their kids to be part of it, but we're saying, "Hell no."

GT: So I take it you're against this policy. {chuckles}

Greg smiles: I didn't say anything.

GT: Well what do you think about this policy?

Greg: I think this policy has done a lot of damage, and that's not just a supposition. You can put real numbers behind that. I don't like to be in the position of explaining to the president of the seminary why my church is whacking infants. But I didn't explain that. I said, "David, I don't understand this anymore than you do." Because there is nothing in LDS theology that I know of that justifies whacking infants; they are pure and sin-free. We are punishing them with this policy.

GT: I think we never answered that other question too. As far as the Second Article of Faith, does it appear that this policy is punishing children for the "sins" of their parents?

Greg: That's what it looks like to me. You're not punishing an infant for its own sins because it's sin-free.

GT: Right.

Greg: Is this a punishment? Yes, it is.

GT: Because there are some who would argue it is not.

Greg: Let them argue it. Because I'll go back to what I said earlier; this is the rite of passage within the LDS tradition, within other Christian traditions, whereby an infant is accepted by the religious community and named. "I give you a name and a blessing."[9] We are denying that to that infant, denying the name and denying the blessing. Is that punishment? Yeah in my book it is.

---

[9] Greg quotes the standard phrasing of the LDS rite of blessing an infant.

The 4 LDS Leadership Vacuums – What Happened?

Introduction

Previously we discussed the gay policy which disallows children of gay parents from receiving blessings, baptisms, or ordinations in the LDS Church. It seems like this policy was started perhaps when President Monson was more incapacitated than he has been in the past. Is there a leadership vacuum? Dr. Greg Prince will talk more about this, and I'll ask if there are similarities between the 1969 policy on blacks. Is that similar to the policy with gays? Check out our conversation…..

The Interview

GT: What I'm seeing here, and tell me if you agree with this perception, it seems to me, and it's funny that you mentioned this all started in 1968, because in 1969, as I understand it from Michael Quinn, there was a vote in the Quorum of Twelve to allow blacks to hold the priesthood and then this vote was later rescinded. It seems like in '68-69, President McKay was more feeble, wasn't really leading the church as much. According to Quinn, and you can tell me if you agree or disagree with this, according to Quinn there seemed to be some jockeying for leadership to lead the church while President McKay was ailing.

In our current day it seems like President Monson, much like President McKay is ailing mentally quite a bit. I've heard rumors that certain members of the quorum kind of sprung this on everybody else and it sounds to me that there are a lot of parallels between 1969 and 2015. Could you comment on that?

Greg: Lester Bush, Brent Rushforth and I published an article a year ago in *Dialogue*,[10] and it was called

"Gerontocracy and the Future of Mormonism."[11] What we did is to go back to 1897, because that was the year the church began to publish their General Conference[12] report, so it's a beginning to end transcript of what went on during the General Conference; all of the discourses, verbatim, whatever statistical reports were given, because we were trying to put objective measurements to fitness for duty for a general authority. That's kind of a euphemistic way of describing it.

But trying to give an objective look at, when did we get to the point where medicine was keeping people alive longer from the neck down than from the neck up basically? What we did is look at all of these General Conference reports, that's more than 100 years' worth times two per year, one thing that became apparent very quickly is there was one group that always spoke at General Conference if they were in town and physically capable of doing so. That was the Q15: Quorum of Twelve plus First Presidency.

The Presiding Bishopric, the Seventies, used to speak in every General Conference before it became a larger bureaucracy, and then when President Kimball re-constituted the First Quorum of Seventy and you had so many Seventies you couldn't identify them anymore, then the Seventies didn't speak at every General Conference and it was during the Kimball administration that we went

---

[10] *Dialogue* is a magazine dedicated to publishing Mormon history.

[11] A preview is found at https://search.proquest.com/openview/fb9374ed40eb0fff43d71a9a7ae51ce4/1?pq-origsite=gscholar&cbl=48252 . Greg's *Radiowest* interview on the topic is available at http://radiowest.kuer.org/post/gerontocracy-and-future-mormonism

[12] LDS Church leaders speak to the entire membership in April and October. These addresses are known by Mormons as General Conference.

from a three-day conference to a two-day conference so that cut it even more.

Without fail, if the Q15 were present and able for duty, they spoke. So we said, alright, let's just take a tally. So we looked at the Q15 for over a hundred years and just filled out this huge database with over 3,000 data points in it and said, what are the trends here?

Up until the 1960s, rarely did a member of that group miss more than one General Conference before they died. Frequently they wouldn't miss any General Conferences. Within the six month interval between General Conferences, they went downhill and died without missing. With President McKay, you had the first time when a church president had a prolonged period where he was not able to stand and deliver a General Conference address. Now that's not to say that he or the others that we measured had dementia; it just said their physical and/or mental constitution was such that they were such that they were not able to stand or even sit at the podium and deliver the address. Either nothing was said, or they would have a surrogate. In the case of President McKay, it was one of his sons who frequently would deliver the address in behalf of his father.

So it's the late 1960s when medicine advanced to the point when it was keeping people alive significantly longer than in the past, but not from the neck up. In the case of President McKay, that period was maybe three or four years. His was a little different situation than the later presidents who had because incapacitation in that he kind of cycled between lucidity and non-lucidity. I interviewed his personal physician in preparation for doing the biography and he said up until just a few weeks before his death there were times when he was perfectly lucid. But it was during that period that there turned out to be this war of the titans between Hugh Brown on the one side, the first counselor in the First Presidency, and Harold B. Lee assisted by Alvin Dyer, who was quite racist, because a letter written to the McKay sons by Sterling McMurrin had recounted in 1968 an interview that McMurrin had with McKay in 1954.

Sterling never talked about this. He felt, because it was a private meeting, he should keep the contents private. But by 1968 with President McKay's health clearly in decline, he wrote this letter to Llewellyn McKay and then sent copies to the other two brothers saying, "I think you need to have this within your family records." He described what those contents had been.

Lawrence McKay, the oldest of the sons, took that letter to his father and said, "This is what we got from Sterling McMurrin. Does this accurately represent what you told him?" And [David] read it and said yes it does.

The main thing that set off the battle of the titans was in 1954, Sterling had said, "Look, I'm being put on trial for my church membership because I am considered a heretic, and there are some thing I just don't buy and one of them is the ban on priesthood ordination of blacks."

President McKay said, "That's a policy, and the time will come when that will change."

Well, he hadn't told other people that. He hadn't even told his counselors or members of the quorum [of Twelve] that during those intervening years. I spoke with Ed Kimball, son of Spencer Kimball and his biographer, twice his biographer, I said, "Was there anything in your father's records that suggested he had had discussions with President McKay on the issue of blacks and the priesthood?"

[Ed] said there was not one thing, so [McKay] had really held it tight. When this letter was sent to the McKay sons, Lawrence McKay showed it to Hugh Brown but Alvin Dyer who was an extra counselor in the First Presidency also got a copy of it and he freaked out and took it to Harold B. Lee. Lee pretty much freaked out because both sides, seeing that McKay considered it a policy, assumed that if it's a policy then it can be changed. That was the good news for Brown. It was the bad news for Lee and for Dyer. So there was some real heavy-duty sparring going on.

I talked to Ed Firmage who was the grandson of Hugh Brown and he was the one who told me, "Yes my grandfather tried to change that administratively, and that's why he was released from the First Presidency after McKay died." But all of that occurred in a period where there was a period of power vacuum. President McKay, even though he was lucid enough to talk to his son and verify the contents of that letter physically didn't have capacity to referee this match or to stop it. It was carried on mostly in private so the general church membership didn't know about it, but it was a real crisis. So that was power vacuum #1.

Power vacuum #2 happened when Spencer Kimball began suffering subdural hemorrhages, and had to have at least, as I recall, two cranial surgeries to remove the blood clots. So his physical and mental capacity began to diminish significantly. His was the second presidency where there had been a prolonged period of incapacitation, about four years. During power vacuum #2 there, you had the dismantling of the Historical

Department, of the history division within the Historical Department. This was Leonard Arrington's franchise, and one wondered how that could happen when Spencer Kimball was so affirming to Leonard of what he was doing, and the answer is when there's a power vacuum, then those who are most capable of filling the vacuum will fill the vacuum.

The way this church is setup, that means who is the next senior guy? If he is sitting as a counselor in the First Presidency, you're likely not to see that much of a blip. If he's sitting in the Quorum of the Twelve, then you may, and the next guy in line was Ezra Taft Benson. So it was Ezra Benson, Mark Peterson, and a junior apostle named Boyd Packer who successfully dismantled the history division and sent the historians packing to BYU.

Power vacuum #3 was with Ezra Taft Benson who was basically totally incapacitated for almost five years, and the efforts by some church leaders to try to deny that resulted directly in the very high profile defection of Steve Benson, one of the grandsons who said, "Look, you're propping up my grandfather and trying to say he's running the church. My grandfather can't even utter a coherent sentence."

Power vacuum #4 is what we're seeing right now. You have seen a diminishing of President Monson's capacity ever since he became church president in 2008. He held one press conference right after he became president. That's been it. If you look at the role he has played in General Conferences, it has been since 2009 since he conducted a session. The last two General Conferences, instead of doing the customary four addresses, he cut down to two and they were basically for those old enough to remember, two and a half minute talks. It's in power vacuum #4 that the Policy emerges. Now that doesn't tell you the details of how these things happened, but it tells you the climate in which they did happen. In each case, it was a power vacuum created by the incapacitation of this living president.

Ailing Church Leaders: "Not Ideal Governance"

The Interview

GT: What do you think the church should do to avoid these types of power vacuums? Or should they? Should they do anything?

Greg: Well, what we showed in our article is that trend continues. It began in the 1960s but it's becoming more frequent within the Q12 [Quorum of Twelve.] Now the Seventies fixed that in the 1970s by introducing the concept of emeritus status. So even though I'm not aware that they ever put it in print publicly,[13] the age of 70 became the age at which members of the First Quorum would become emeritus. So for them, that fixed the problem.

GT: It fixed the problem for the Seventies.

Greg: For the Seventies. I spoke with one of the Seventies who was involved in that first position paper going back to the 1970s where they established emeritus

---

[13] This *Deseret News* article refers to a policy on the LDS website, but the link does not contain the quote referenced. The LDS Church website [https://www.lds.org/church/leaders/quorums-of-the-seventy]indicates that "members of the First Quorum of the Seventy are called to serve until the age of 70, at which time they are given emeritus status (similar to being released). Members of the Second Quorum of the Seventy typically serve for three to five years; after this time, they are released."

Prior to 1978, general authorities served for the rest of their lives, according to Elder Bruce C. Hafen, who was given emeritus status in 2010.

See https://www.deseretnews.com/article/865563554/Emeritus-general-authorities-welcome-the-chance-to-practice-what-theyve-preached.html [status] and said, "Did you ever suggest this to the Quorum of Twelve?"

He chuckled and said, "That was above our pay grade but we certainly opened the door if they had wanted to walk through."

GT: Why do you think that they don't offer [emeritus status]? I remember pope, I'm trying to remember what his name was, Pope Benedict resigned a few years ago...

Greg: Yes, that's right.

GT: ... paving the way for Pope Francis. He's still alive.

Greg: Yes. If it happens with Francis then it will have established a precedent that they probably will stick with, but we have not taken that step. Now the Catholic Church differs from the Mormon Church not in previously having the church leader serve until death. Both of us did that until Pope Benedict, but the difference is that the Catholic Church does not have a succession policy that relies strictly on seniority. Ours does, and so you can look at Q15[14] and list with absolute certainty who is going to be next. The only thing that will change that is if somebody dies before they reach the president's chair.

GT: Such as President Packer.[15]

Greg: Yes, that's right. So I'm sure that's part of the discussion at that level. [They think], "The Lord called me to this position." They know what the sequence of events

---

[14] Shorthand for Quorum of 12, plus 3 members of First Presidency.

[15] Boyd K. Packer was serving as President of the Quorum of Twelve. He was the most senior apostle and would have been next in line to succeed President Monson, but he died July 3, 2015. Russell M. Nelson replaced Packer and is next in line to replace Monson. Dallin Oaks is third in line.

is. But we looked at this not through political eyes so much as medical eyes. What we call the zone of dementia begins roughly in the mid-80s. By the time you get to your late 80s, you've got almost a 50-50 chance of showing signs of dementia. That zone hasn't moved. What's happened is that more people are moving through that zone because they are living to an older age.

We have been much more successful at keeping the body alive than in keeping the mind alive, so this has kind of a cascade effect. More of them are moving into the zone of dementia, and because they are all on average living longer than the predecessors, it means that the sitting church president in each case on average, will live to an older age than his predecessor.

In the case of President Hinckley, he was an outlier because he not only lived to age 97, but he had a full deck of cards. He had his fastball until hours before he died. That's highly unusual. So the usual outcome will be that the sitting president will live to an older age than his predecessor, which means that his successor will be older upon sitting in the president's chair than his predecessor was. You see the ripple effect of this.

So, if you're just looking at this from a medical standpoint, it's inevitable that incapacitation of an LDS Church president will be both more frequent and longer lasting. In a fast-paced, complex world with a growing church, that may not give you the ideal governance. So the question is, what do you do about it?

What we did about it is to say look. Here's the medicine involved in this, period. If they choose to address the situation at some point, it's their call. But what we can say with a high level of confidence, because we looked at this through the eyes of medicine is, this is the situation. It's going to happen more frequently, and last longer.

GT: Do you ever see this policy changing?

Greg: I see virtually anything changing because I have seen everything change. I'm not aware of a single LDS doctrine of any significance that from 1830 forward has gone completely unchanged. You'd think a lot of them would, but it turns out, no there were some substantial changes in many cases very early on. If you just look at the First Vision narratives, you see the evolution of Joseph Smith's theology of deity, and it's taking place in a very rapid fashion and in a very dramatic fashion.

It wasn't just nibbling at the periphery. He was going through evolutionary leaps in the way that he portrayed the godhead. That was reflected in his subsequent retellings of the story of the First Vision. Each time he told it anew, it incorporated the then current version of his theology of deity. That's why those different versions are telling different stories, because they became theological narratives rather than historical narratives.

GT: Wow, there's so many directions I could go here. The one thing I want to jump back to, let's jump back to President Kimball for a minute.

There's a story, and I'm sure most people have heard it, about a guy whose house is flooding and some police come by and say hey, you need to get out of your house. He says, "No, God will protect me."

The waters keep rising and he ends up on his roof and a helicopter comes and says, "Do you need help?"

"No, God will protect me."

The man drowns, and he gets up to heaven and he says, "God, why didn't you help me?"

God says, "Well I sent a helicopter and the police. What more did you want?"

Some people have looked at the incapacitation of prophets. One of the things that I found interesting in Edward Kimball's biography, was President Kimball would ask, "God, why are you putting me through all this?"

Some people may say, "Well, God is sending you a message. You're not getting it." I guess my question is, I understand that the apostles believe that God has called them to [the apostleship], and I do believe that God has called them to that. But isn't there a time when it seems like they should recognize, like this man on the roof, maybe this is a sign that maybe I should retire. What do you think of that?

Greg: Well they changed the succession policy three times in the first century of the church's existence. The first time was when the first apostle died, because the initial Quorum of Twelve had seniority on the basis of chronological age. When a new apostle came in, they decided if he is older than the other ones, and Lyman Wight was; he would have been the senior apostle based on age, but he was the newest apostle, then they changed it and said, no, seniority is based on how long you have been an apostle.

Then they changed it again because Orson Pratt and Orson Hyde, in a time when you could be excommunicated at the drop of a hat, had been excommunicated and dropped from the quorum, and then just weeks later were reinstated to church membership and to the Quorum of Twelve.

GT: Now were they excommunicated by Joseph Smith?

Greg: Yes. Near the end of Brigham Young's life, he decided—P.S. He and Orson Pratt had sparred bitterly

and openly for years on doctrinal issues, he could see
that the next in line was Orson Pratt, so he changed it
and said, no, the clock started anew.

GT interrupts: Brigham Young changed it.

Greg: Yes, when they came back into the quorum, so it
bumped them down several notches. It meant that both
of them, who would have become president, didn't
become president. Then right at the turn of the century,
you're tempted to say it was payback because it involved
Brigham Young's son, Brigham Jr. Pay your money, take
your choice.

But he was the senior apostle and Lorenzo Snow was the
president. They made the decision: Brigham ordained
you an apostle when there wasn't a vacancy in the
Quorum of Twelve. That's happened 11 or 12 times in
the history of the church; the most recent was Alvin Dyer,
who never did go into the Quorum of Twelve, but he was
an apostle.[16]

Brigham Jr. had been ordained an apostle but then
Joseph F. Smith was ordained an apostle subsequent to
that but was also admitted to the Quorum of Twelve. So

---

[16] From Wikipedia. "Alvin Rulon Dyer (January 1, 1903 – March 6, 1977) was an
apostle in The Church of Jesus Christ of Latter-day Saints (LDS Church) and
served as a member of the church's First Presidency from 1968 to 1970.

Born in Salt Lake City, Utah, Dyer was ordained as an apostle on October 5,
1967, (but was not added as a member of the Quorum of the Twelve Apostles)
and subsequently was set apart as a counselor in the First Presidency to church
president David O. McKay. After McKay's death in 1970, Dyer was returned to a
position as an Assistant to the Twelve Apostles, and later to the First Quorum
of the Seventy when it was reconstituted in 1976. Dyer is the only person in the
history of the LDS Church to serve in the First Quorum of Seventy after having
been ordained to the office of Apostle." See
https://en.wikipedia.org/wiki/Alvin_R._Dyer

that third change was, no it's not how long you've been
an apostle, it's how long you've been in the Quorum of
Twelve, thereby taking Brigham Young, Jr. out of the
president's chair. Otherwise he would have been church
president as well. So it wasn't just a theoretical thing
that they were doing.

They have changed this significantly in the past. Are they
going to change it again? I don't know. But to argue
that they can't change anything, ignores the history
because they have.

GT: That's very interesting. Let's move back. This is great.

Greg: You're never going to be able to give a title to this.
It's going all over the place.

GT chuckles: It is going all over the place, but it's nice that I can chop it
up into pieces. One of the things I wanted to talk to you about,
especially since you did the biography on David O. McKay[17] was the
temple ship. Can you, for people who haven't read your book, tell us a
little bit about the temple ship?

Greg: This was in the latter part of the 1960s, and there
was a serious suggestion that the Church buy an ocean
liner and retrofit it to be a floating temple. That was at a
time when we had very few temples, particularly outside
of North America and large population centers near port
cities all over the world. So the idea was that if we can't
build temples everywhere, at least we could take the
temple experience to people where they were by having it
in this ocean liner. When I was writing the McKay
biography, I described this. I couldn't resist putting in
the phrase, "They floated the idea of this." The editor
took it out.

---

[17] See http://amzn.to/2AjUSR5

GT chuckles: That's too bad.

Greg: But it was discussed for several months.

GT: How serious do you think that was?

Greg: I think it was a very serious concept that they were doing. It was about that same time I think that there was also a fair amount of talk about, do we need full-size temples everywhere? Can we do with a smaller temple? In fact it did go that direction. President Hinckley gets the credit for that, but that actually was discussed and proposed well before he became the church president.

There had even been discussions, either could we take part of an existing stake center, or build onto a stake center, and have a really super compact temple that could be opened as necessary in order to give temple ordinances to people who lived in really faraway places, people who didn't have the resources to travel all the way to wherever the temple was. When I went to Brazil as a missionary in 1967, the entire continent of South America had to go to Arizona for the nearest temple. Now if you're in the southern tip of Chile, think about that.

GT: Wow. That's probably 10,000 miles.

Greg: Not that many, but it's more than a couple of thousand miles.[18] It made sense logistically. They could have done it.

GT: What killed the idea?

---

[18] The distance from southern Chile to Tempe, Arizona is approximately 6700 miles by air.

Greg: I don't know who finally put the spike in the heart of it. The McKay records didn't say anything about that. It just fizzled.

GT: It seems like, if I remember right, that Alvin Dyer referenced a scripture in the Doctrine and Covenants about Satan being on the waters.[19] Do you remember that?

Greg: Yeah I remember. Dyer had a lot of pet notions, some of them loosely grounded in fact, some of them not grounded at all in fact.

GT: Do you think that weighed in there?

Greg: I don't know.

GT: Because he was in the First Presidency. You would think his opinion would hold a fair amount of weight.

Greg: When I mentioned the ocean liner to a temple president who was just finishing his term, and he didn't give me all of the details, he said there actually had been a discussion at a high level of retrofitting a 747 and making a flying temple.

GT: Oh really! I hadn't heard that one.

Greg: He said, "You could do it that way. It would work."

GT: Wow.

Greg: The first one didn't float and the second one didn't fly.

____

[19] D&C 61:19 reads, "I, the Lord, have decreed, and the destroyer rideth upon the face thereof, and I revoke not the decree." See https://www.lds.org/scriptures/dc-testament/dc/61.19

GT chuckles: That sounds like a great title! I had not heard about the jumbo jet temple. That's interesting.

Early LDS Priesthood: Similar to Ancient Christianity?

The Interview

GT: One of the things that I really wanted to talk to you about was the evolution of priesthood. We've talked a little bit about that. You've talked a little bit about some of the changes in succession and even the First Vision. Let's talk a little bit about the organization of the church. It seems to me, I've heard Michael Quinn say that I believe the first few offices were Elder, Priest, and Teacher. Now we typically think of elder as in the Melchizedek Priesthood, but it seems like it was a lot more muddled back then. Can you talk a little bit about the early organization of the priesthood?

Greg: Yes, I think you need to start by backing up to the time when there wasn't even a church and look at phases that Joseph Smith went through. The earliest phase was there wasn't even talk of the church. There wasn't even talk of authority. When he had his First Vision, if you looked at the earliest version of that as likely being the most authentic historically, it had nothing to do with churches.

He said in his account of it in 1832, [he] already knew from studying the bible that all the churches were wrong, which is diametrically opposed to what the canonized version says. So he went to the grove for personal forgiveness, and that's what that account said. The Lord appeared and said Joseph had been forgiven; end of story, bye, bye. [There was] no hint that there would be a church in his future.

When you start to get into the Moroni narratives, then you have implicit authority, meaning that people around Joseph believed that something extraordinary was going on, and when he got the plates, they saw that something extraordinary was going on, and nobody challenged his authority to do it. Towards the end of the translation process, they become concerned about having authority to perform ordinances, baptism being the primary one. Now they never worried about that up until this point. So that's what drove him to seek explicit authority. That was the authority that they described in the restoration of what became known as the Aaronic Priesthood, but it wasn't known as that for another six years. Neither was Melchizedek Priesthood called Melchizedek Priesthood until 1835 sometime.

What they were looking for was authority, and the earliest church structure mirrored that of the Book of Mormon. The Nephite Christian Church described in the latter chapters of the Book of Mormon had only three offices: teachers, priests, and elders, and there's minimal description in there, but there was a differentiation between the teachers and priests on the one hand, and elders on the other hand. The word "priesthood" was not used. In fact "priesthood" was more likely to be interpreted as "priestcraft" in the Book of Mormon, the evil priests.

GT: Oh really.

Greg: It was authority. What differentiated the elders from the other two guys was that the elders could confer the Holy Spirit, and priests and teachers could not. So you had the idea of three offices, but two levels of authority within the Book of Mormon. David Whitmer, who wrote later but much later *An Address to All*

Believers in Christ,[20] complained that Joseph took it beyond that. He said we had everything we needed. We had the pure church when we had only those three offices.

Now that's a little disingenuous because Whitmer still bought into it for a long time after that. His complaining was when he wrote that pamphlet in the 1870s. But nonetheless, he affirmed what we can verify from other sources including the Book of Mormon. In the earliest church there were just those three offices.

If you look at the Far West record, which is basically the minute book of the early church general conferences, in the first conference that is recorded in June 1830, there are only three offices to which people are ordained: teachers, priests, and elders. You have two others appended in 1831: those were deacons and bishops.

Now if you look at the current section 20 of the Doctrine & Covenants, there is a lengthy paragraph and it says, "the duty of the elders is to…", and it gives the description. "The duty of the priests is to…", it gives the description. "The duty of the teachers is to…and the deacons are to assist them in all manners." It looks like an appendix, and it is. If you look back at the various iterations of what became section 20, deacons weren't there initially.

GT: Oh really, so that's an addition. Wow.

Greg: That's an addition made in an 1829 document. It's called the *Articles & Covenants* of the Church,[21] which

---

[20] See http://amzn.to/2jDqdEj
[21] More information can be found at https://history.lds.org/article/articles-and-covenants-of-the-church?lang=eng

was written by Oliver Cowdery. It describes the basic church structure. It enumerates those three offices and gives those job descriptions. The office of bishop is apart from those three, the priests, teachers, deacons, and you don't get bishops and deacons until after the arrival of in New York in late 1830 of Sidney Rigdon.

Sidney Rigdon came from the Campbellite tradition. He split with Alexander Campbell over the issue of gifts of the spirit. Campbell said those were fine in ancient times. There's no need for them now in the modern church even though Campbell said we are a restoration of the primitive church. Whereas Rigdon said, no, the gifts of the spirit are in fact signs of the true church. That was the essence of why they split. At the time he left the Campbellite tradition Sidney was a Campbellite bishop.

GT: Oh.

Greg: Furthermore, if you look at the newspaper that the Campbellite tradition, Alexander Campbell published prior to the *Millennial Harbinger*, which I think was 1830 or '31, the earlier version was called *The Christian Baptist*. It went back to about 1823. It says in there, there are only two offices that are legitimate within the Christian Church. They are bishop and deacon.

GT: Oh really. What about apostle? Those are mentioned. No?

Greg shakes his head: They did not have those offices within the Campbellite movement.

GT: I don't understand how they would leave out apostles. That seems strange to me.

Greg: I report the history. I don't make it. {chuckles}

So you have those two being brought in simultaneous with the arrival of Sidney Rigdon who was a Campbellite bishop. When the first bishop was ordained, Edward Partridge, would you not have thought the first elder in the church would ordain him? But he didn't. Edward Partridge was ordained a bishop by Sidney Rigdon.

GT: Was he in the First Presidency then?

Greg: No.

GT: Oh really. Ok.

Greg: This thing gets cobbled together over time. The Seventies don't come in until 1835, and that's after the failure of Zion's Camp. Apostle gets reinvented because there were apostles before the church was officially founded. There were a dozen of them. There were newspaper accounts of the Mormonites[22] talking about having twelve apostles, but they didn't have any discrete function. They didn't function as a unit and then they disappeared. Then in 1835, the Quorum of Twelve Apostles was organized. They look back on that as their founding year but it really wasn't. They were there five or six years before that.

Then you have the office of Patriarch that kind of comes out of nowhere, but that's something Joseph can kind of give to his father and then it becomes passed down from father to son on a general level and eventually it is disseminated into the stakes. If you look at all this looking forward through history, rather than looking back and trying to harmonize it and put it into neat packages, you see that it's messy. It's evolutionary. It doesn't

____

[22] Early accounts referred to Mormons as Mormonites.

correspond to anything ancient in any discernable fashion.

You can make the claim that this is a restoration of the primitive church structure, but you can't make that stick. Yes those offices are recognized both in the New Testament. It's about as far as you can take it. The concept of a dual-tiered priesthood existing within an early Christian church isn't there. It's taking parts of Old Testament theology, parts of New Testament theology, doing some cherry-picking, and eventually settling in pretty much on where we have it now.

But we call some things offices because we call them offices. Other things that we could call offices, we don't call offices because we don't call them offices. This sounds like a really stupid way of saying it but it's as good of a definition as you're going to find within the Mormon tradition. Something that's called an office because somebody decided to call it an office; stake president could easily be described as an ordained office. If you look at a chain of command, there it is. You've got an ordained bishop, but you have a set apart stake president, and then you have an ordained Seventy above him. Go figure. But it's because somebody decided at some point, ok we'll set those apart, so these are offices that we ordain to and these are offices that we don't ordain to.

GT: Even that's a little bit murky because as I recall, and I think this is in your book, the Relief Society President Emma [Smith] was ordained as president, right?

Greg: Sure.

GT: The "ordained" and "set apart," those words were often interchanged, but they are not anymore.

Greg: Not anymore. No we get really hung up over that. Similarly, an ordinance is something that we call an ordinance. There are some ordinances that we used to have that we quietly did away with.

GT: Such as?

Greg: Outside of the temple and various other circumstances, washing the feet is one. We don't do baptism for the restoration of health anymore. Those are ordinances and they were practiced broadly. The newest kid on the block, would you like to take a guess as to what and when?

GT: The Endowment I guess. I'm not sure. I don't know.

Greg: Dedication of graves, 1976.

GT: That's only since '76?

Greg: Yes, if you go back to the '20s and before that when it's mentioned in the general handbook, initially it says it is not an ordinance, and it doesn't need to be a priesthood holder who does it. Then a few years later it is not an ordinance but it would be nice to have a priesthood holder to do it. Then it's not an ordinance but it needs to be done by a priesthood holder. Then finally, this is a Melchizedek Priesthood ordinance. That was 1976.

GT: Oh really. That was 1976. Because we have a similar sort of thing with women being able to bless the sick; can you take about that evolution over the years?

Greg: Well that was a devolution.

GT: A devolution. {chuckles}

Greg: Because it was there at a very early time period
that they were blessing each other and blessing others for
the restoration of health. It wasn't until the early 20th
century that they were to back off that. That really
coincided with the effort to try to get the men to function
in their priesthood quorums because by the turn of the
20th century, and even before that, most of the quorums
didn't function in any meaningful fashion.

So if you look at any priesthood manuals, particularly in
the '20s and '30s, the focus year after year was to try to
get quorums to function. Try to get men to understand
what priesthood is and to try to do something about it.
Well if the women are doing the same thing that you want
the men to be doing, that muddies the water. So the
answer was, women quit doing it.

GT: Oh really? Is that why?

Greg: Yes.

GT: You think that's why. So that's why the church took away blessing
of the sick from the women and essentially gave it to males.

Greg: Yes. If you go back to one of the early issues of
Sunstone, the cover article on that is called A Gift Given,
a Gift Taken.[23] Linda Newell is one of the authors. I had
breakfast with Linda this morning.

GT: Oh really? I need to interview her. {chuckles}

Greg: But we still have women in the temple who are set
apart/not ordained to perform non-ordinances, which are

____

[23] A PDF of the article can be found at
https://www.sunstonemagazine.com/pdf/029-16-25.pdf

the same as things that men who are ordained, perform in the temple that we call ordinances.

GT: So that brings up another question. Let's talk about women and the priesthood.

Greg: I would like to quote a current national president. "Who knew it could be so complicated?"[24]

GT chuckles: So it seems like Michael Quinn has made an argument that women actually do hold the priesthood in the LDS Church but most don't recognize it because we don't ordain them to a priesthood office like we do men, in that when they do receive their temple endowment, they do receive a form of priesthood. Then the question is, what do they do with this priesthood? Nothing, except for the temple.

Greg: Well it all hinges on semantics. What are you going to call priesthood? Depending on how you define it then you can say if you define it this way then they have part of what we call priesthood. But if you define it that way, you say no.

GT: That goes to right where I was going to say.

Greg: It's an argument I am just not even interested in getting into.

GT chuckles: Darn! I wanted to do that.

----

[24] Donald Trump had campaigned on a pledge to repeal the Affordable Care Act, also known as Obamacare, which is a highly complex law designed to allow more Americans to afford health insurance. After further study in office he said, "I have to tell you, it's an unbelievably complex subject," he told the reporters. "Nobody knew that health care could be so complicated." He was widely ridiculed for his lack of understanding of the issue because almost everyone knew it was complicated except for him apparently. See http://www.slate.com/blogs/moneybox/2017/02/27/trump_says_nobody_kne w_health_care_could_be_so_complicated.html

Greg: Because I don't see any point to it!

GT: Well because Jonathan Stapley has made an argument kind of against Quinn that says that no women have ever thought that they held the priesthood. Yes they did anoint, even with oil, so they blessed the sick, but no woman, despite what some patriarchal blessings say, and I believe that's in your book[25] as well about some women that were ordained to bless the sick I believe. Can you weigh in on that? Did early women think that they held priesthood and could bless the sick?

Greg: I doubt that they were hung up about it. I haven't seen any documents that would say, "Hey, we hold the priesthood." I don't think they were a bit concerned about nomenclature. I think they were doing what they did and they didn't care about tidying it up.

It was later into the 20th century when we began to draw those boundary lines in bold, black ink. Women are over here, they don't have the priesthood. Men are over here, and they do have the priesthood. I think if you go back into the 19th century, particularly the closer you get to the origins of the church, the fuzzier you would see that line.

To try to apply the standards of today to the reality of then is a fool's errand. I know a lot of people interested in arguing about that but fine. Go argue. It doesn't make any difference. The most difficult thing for a historian is to recreate the environment of the history of the incident he is writing about so that the reader can breathe that air. That's extremely difficult to do, but it's essential to get as close to that as you can. Otherwise you're going to give a distorted view of that history. I don't see many of our historians who have done a very good job of recreating that.

---

[25] Greg's book is called *Priesthood from on High* and is found at http://amzn.to/2nqcCFM

Naturalistic Explanation for Word of Wisdom?

We're continuing our conversation about revelation in the LDS Church. One of Mormonism's most important and well-known revelations deals with the Word of Wisdom, Mormonism's health code. Dr. Greg Prince talks about a naturalistic view of how that revelation was received. I think it's pretty surprising. We'll also tell some stories about President McKay. Did he prefer Coke or Pepsi? Check out our conversation. Another thing that gets short shrift in the Word of Wisdom is about meat and hot drinks. What does Greg have to say about that? It's going to be a very fun conversation. I hope you join us.....

The Interview

Greg: If you look at the Word of Wisdom, how many people have recreated what the conventional wisdom of 1833 was in the United States was about temperance?

GT: I just heard Lach MacKay[26] give a wonderful Sunday School lesson on that very topic which I thought was fascinating, talking about the difference between temperance and prohibition. He made the case that those are different and that the Word of Wisdom really doesn't forbid alcohol. That's really more of a Heber J. Grant[27] thing. Once

---

[26] Lachlan MacKay is currently an apostle of the Community of Christ. He will be featured in an upcoming interview and has some very interesting insights about the Word of Wisdom.

[27] Heber J. Grant served as seventh LDS President from 1918-1945. During his administration, the United States repealed the 18th amendment to the Constitution in December 1933. Grant was upset because Utah became the 36th and deciding state to vote for repealing Prohibition, paving the way for legalization of alcohol.

again, just like with the gay issue,[it was] a reaction to the rescission of Prohibition.

Greg: You have, I think, three phases of Word of Wisdom. Phase one was when Joseph writes it down but nobody pays much attention to it. Phase two is when the saints get out to the Salt Lake Valley and hard cash is scarce and Brigham is trying to conserve it and so he comes down hard on the importing of luxury goods from the east because that takes scarce cash out of Utah and doesn't replace it. What are those scarce goods? Primarily tea, coffee, some tobacco, and distilled liquor; so that's when he really came down hard.

This is an article in the very first issue of *BYU Studies* written by Leonard Arrington called the *Economic Interpretation of the Word of Wisdom*.[28] It is a very strong, credible case that that era of Word of Wisdom enforcement was done for the very pragmatic reason of trying to preserve capital within the Utah Territory.

Then you get into the Heber Grant era where he just becomes a stickler, and takes a hard line on it and makes pronouncements that would have had no context when the Word of Wisdom was given because, for instance, there was no such thing as a carbonated drink or even a cold drink. If there had been iced drinks, probably the Word of Wisdom would have said no hot drinks and no iced drinks because the whole notion was temperance, moderation. Find the center ground, the comfort zone and stay there. Don't go this way, don't go that way.

I've got in my library about seven linear feet of publications that pre-date February 27, 1833 that deal

---

[28] Can be downloaded for free at
https://byustudies.byu.edu/content/economic-interpretation-word-wisdom

with temperance. To the smallest detail what's in the Word of Wisdom, that's been out there for years. You will hear people still who say the Word of Wisdom proves Joseph was a prophet because it was a hundred years ahead of its time. It wasn't even a day ahead of its time. It reflected what everybody already knew. This was the air that they breathed.

The Temperance Movement kicked in in 1826 because there was an epidemic of drunkenness in the United States. The consumption of distilled liquor over a 30 year period had tripled on a per capita basis. Drunkenness became a national security issue. That's why the American Temperance Society was formed in 1826.

GT: Tripled between what year and what year?

Greg: In the 30 years prior to 1826

GT: Ok.

Greg: So the Temperance Movement was focused initially was focused mostly on alcohol but not all of it. All of the other things including the good and the bad were out there in the public press in the general public press. This wasn't in medical journals exclusively saying here's what you want to do to have a temperate life. It's all in there.

Well if you don't recreate that environment to the best that you can, then people are clueless as to what the real context of the Word of Wisdom was. It said "strong drinks" because that's what was getting guys into trouble. It was distilled spirits. It wasn't wine.[29] It wasn't beer.

---

[29] D&C 89: 5-7 says "5 That inasmuch as any man drinketh wine or strong drink among you, behold it is not good, neither meet in the sight of your Father, only in assembling yourselves together to offer up your sacraments before him.

In fact Danish beer was still ok for the Danish general authorities through the early decades of the 20th century. They decided (the First Presidency) they wouldn't deny them a temple recommend because they were still drinking Danish beer because that was mother's milk to them. They didn't have the heart to pull the plug on that one, until Grant did it finally.

GT: It wasn't a reaction to Utah, of all states.

Greg: Yeah. When they are saying "strong drinks," it didn't mean "anything with alcohol in it." It meant distilled spirits.

GT: Vodka.

Greg: It didn't mean wine. It didn't mean beer. When they said "hot drinks," it mean drinks that were hot. It wasn't what was in them.

GT: Including hot chocolate?

Greg: People didn't drink hot chocolate. They only drank two hot drinks: coffee and tea. But it wasn't the content, it was the temperature. It moved you out of that zone of moderation, out of temperance. Later they decided it's because of caffeine. And then they got into this squabble back in the '40s. Ok if we have Sanka which was the first decaffeinated coffee, are we ok?

Hmmm, they kind of went back and forth and never really took a hard line on it. Then we get into subsequent

---

6 And, behold, this should be wine, yea, pure wine of the grape of the vine, of your own make.

7 And, again, strong drinks are not for the belly, but for the washing of your bodies." See https://www.lds.org/scriptures/dc-testament/dc/89

decades and for some of the Orthodox, they won't touch a caffeinated Coke, but they will take a non-caffeinated Coke and an Excedrin, and that's fine, which has more caffeine than Coke does.

GT: I've actually heard—my wife does not drink any caffeine unless she gets a migraine, and it cures her migraines, which would be Excedrin as well I guess.

Greg: Yes. The same thing about fresh vegetables, grains, produce in its season;[30] well that was a good recommendation then. It still is. Red meats: that takes you out of your temperance zone because red meat will stimulate you.[31] You don't want to be over stimulated because you're moving out of the zone. Except if it's cold outside then you need a little extra stimulation. If there's a famine in the land, you need a little extra stimulation.[32] Alright, then bring the red meat in there. See!

But if you understand all of that and you understand that was the conventional wisdom, that's what the people in the streets heard about and believed and to a large extent followed, then you see then the Word of Wisdom is just kind of extending that same recommendation to the Mormons. It didn't take it any further than the American Temperance Society had taken it.

----

[30] D&C 89:11 says "11 Every herb in the season thereof, and every fruit in the season thereof; all these to be used with prudence and thanksgiving." Verse 14 says, "All grain is ordained for the use of man and of beasts, to be the staff of life, not only for man but for the beasts of the field, and the fowls of heaven, and all wild animals that run or creep on the earth;" See https://www.lds.org/scriptures/dc-testament/dc/89
[31] Verse 13 says "12 Yea, flesh also of beasts and of the fowls of the air, I, the Lord, have ordained for the use of man with thanksgiving; nevertheless they are to be used sparingly;"
[32] Verse 15 says "15 And these hath God made for the use of man only in times of famine and excess of hunger."

Lester Bush first pointed out to me decades ago, he said, "You know if the Lord had wanted to save lives with the Word of Wisdom, why didn't He say 'boil your water?'" Because until the cigarette making machine was invented in the first decade of the 20th century, the Word of Wisdom didn't save lives. Before that when you had to roll your own. People didn't smoke enough for long enough period because they tended to die of infectious diseases that they were getting lung cancer. What was killing them was mostly water-borne bacteria, which could have been killed if they had boiled their water. Oh well.

GT: This is interesting to hear because it sounds like a very naturalistic explanation for the Word of Wisdom.

Greg: Yes it is.

GT: Some would say, is that really revelation then, or is that just the thinking of the day?

Greg: Well you get into the circular argument on that. Is something revelation because we call it revelation, or is the nature of the something what later qualifies it as being revelation? If you're looking for the splitting the ceiling and the voice of the Lord dropping through-type revelation, how many instances of that do we have within the LDS Church tradition?

GT: Not very many.

Greg: Any? Even the revelation on priesthood, it's not that kind. It's not the voice of God penetrating the temple. Yes it is described by some who were there as a Pentecostal experience. It's different though. So what is the nature of revelation? That turns out to be a very difficult thing to pin down. One thing that you can pretty much say across the board is revelation is more process than event.

In the words of Stephen Gould, the biologist, the evolutionary biologist, he described evolution as punctuated equilibrium. You have kind of a steady-state and then you have some cataclysmic events, and you have these spikes of evolution. That turns out not to have held up the way that he would have to have it hold up, but it's an interesting image and I think that the reality in our historical record says that's a good model to explain of the things we've gone through. There's a process that's pretty much steady-state and then it may be punctuated by an event here that is a game changer. Look at some of the earliest days of the church and how the visions changed things in pretty short order like the vision of the three degrees of glory,[33] or the later vision of the Celestial Kingdom.[34]

GT: Alright, the last thing I want to talk about as far as Word of Wisdom is concerned, can you tell the story about President McKay and both Coke and rum cake? {chuckles} I think that's a great story.

Greg: He loves rum cake. That's that story. {chuckles} The story about Coke is that when there was still the Valley Music Hall up in Bountiful, which now is a multi-stake center.

GT: Elder Ballard used to own it, didn't he?

Greg: It was. It was one of several built across the country all built at the same time, all built by the same company. It was a theater in the round. There was one in Maryland that was torn down several years after we

---

[33] See D&C 76 at https://www.lds.org/scriptures/dc-testament/dc/76
[34] See D&C 137 at https://www.lds.org/scriptures/dc-testament/dc/137

moved out there but we went to a couple of events there and it was pretty much a clone of the one we have out here.

The guy who told me this was a BYU student at the time that he was doing publicity for the theater and they had invited the McKays to a performance there. So it was his job to pick up the McKays, take them there. He got them seated before the crowd came in and said, "I'd be happy to get you some refreshments now, but I have to apologize for one thing. That is, by contract the paper cups that we use for our soft drinks are Coca-Cola cups. I can get you root beer, I can get you orange, I can get you Sprite, whatever."

He said President McKay looked up at him and said, "What's on the cup doesn't matter so long as what's in the cup is a Coke."

Now, that's what's in the book.[35] Before the book was published, I was chatting with one of the secretaries who had worked in President McKay's office. She was still alive because she went to work for him right after she got off her mission. She was much younger than the other secretaries in that office. I gave her whatever chapter it was that had that Coke anecdote in it. I gave it to her and I was a little nervous because [she] was a very conservative woman. She read that and she said, "That's not correct."

I said, "What do you mean it's not correct? You know the guy who gave me that story!"

---

[35] Prince wrote the biography, *David O. McKay and the Rise of Modern Mormonism*. See http://amzn.to/2B2JWlX

Then she said, "Well let me tell you. I was up in the apartment with President McKay one time." He said, "Would you go into the other room in the kitchen and get me a soda. It's in the refrigerator."

She said, "Certainly. I walked in and opened the refrigerator and there was a whole shelf full of Pepsi."

GT chuckles: So President McKay was a Pepsi man!

Greg: I think he was versatile.

GT chuckles: Ok so there's that other story about rum cake.

Greg: Yeah, he was at a party and he enjoyed rum cake. If you can eat it with a fork it's ok I guess.

GT chuckles: If I recall from your book, I think this is the quote. It said something to the effect that there's no problem with eating alcohol, it's drinking it that is the problem. {chuckles}

Greg: Yeah same idea; eat it with a fork. You're ok.

GT chuckles: I just think most people—and the funny thing is now BYU is finally allowing Coke on campus.

Greg: Yeah suddenly there's a demand for it where there wasn't a demand before. {chuckles}

GT chuckles: I understand there's still not a demand for it at BYU-Idaho though. It's still prohibited. I guess the BYU-Idaho students need to start picketing or something.

Greg: It might be part of the application that they file when they want to go there. Do you have an appetite for Coca-Cola with caffeine? If they say no, then they get sent to BYU-Idaho. Maybe that's what's going on?

GT chuckles: There was one other quote. We'll just finish this off there. It seems like there was a question about chocolate. Chocolate has caffeine in it.

Greg: Oh John Widtsoe wanted there to be a ban on chocolate. His wife Leah Widtsoe was a health fanatic. The two of them wrote a book on the Word of Wisdom, and I think it was a priesthood manual back in the '30s. The anecdotal story that I have heard from more than one source is that when Widtsoe suggested that maybe this should be put on the prohibited list, McKay's response was "Do you want to take all the fun out of life John?"

GT chuckles: I love that.

Greg: It was a much more relaxed church.

GT: Sometimes I wish it was a little bit more relaxed now.

Greg: These things tend to be cyclical, although the length of the cycles sometimes are way too long for our patience.

GT: Yes.

When Did LDS Start Ordaining Youth?

The Interview

GT: Alright, the last topic that I wanted to talk to you about was a little bit about—in fact I was talking to Jim Vun Cannon. He's a member of the First Presidency of the Remnant Church of Jesus Christ of Latter-day Saints. He actually asked me a question. He said, "Why do you ordain young men to the priesthood?" Because it didn't used to be the case, especially in the early days of the church.

Greg: That's right.

GT: Can you talk about how that changed and why that changed?

Greg: My recollection is that I think it was 1904. Joseph Keeler published a book under the direction of the First Presidency, that's stated in the preface, and I'm blocking on what the name of it was but it was almost a general handbook of instructions. I think it was *Lesser Priesthood and Church Governance*[36] (or something like that.) It went through two editions and he changed the title later on.

But as far as I can tell, that was the first time when ages were prescribed for ordination into the Aaronic Priesthood. Initially it was 12, 15, and 18 for Deacon, Teacher, and Priest. Then later that was revised and became 12, 14, and 16. Elder at one point was 21, and then they backed it up to 19, and when missionaries were going out at 19 instead of 21. Then the missionaries

---

[36] See http://amzn.to/2B9f3m6

were going out at 18 and they backed it up to 18, so that's where we are now.

In the 19th century, the boys weren't part of priesthood. The Teachers were really the glue that held the church together, because the Teachers were now what we would call the home teachers, but they were adult men. If you go back and look at the records of wards in the 19th century, one of the richest records, and a fascinating record is the record of Teachers meetings. I looked through the 8th ward, because Elijah Sheets was the bishop of that ward for 48 years. I think it's safe to say that record will never be broken.

GT chuckles: I would think so.

Greg: But they held that meeting every week. They would go down the roster of the ward continually and say, "How was sister so-and-so doing?"

"Well she needs a cord of wood."

"Ok you guys make sure the cord of wood is delivered to her to help her get through the winter."

"How is brother so-and-so?"

It really was, as I just said, the glue I think that held the church together. But it was all the adult men who were the ordained Teachers. That's what they did. It wasn't until you get into the 20th century that you have the notion of boys now doing this stuff, and then pretty much they had to decide: what do we have boys doing?

Well the priests were blessing the sacrament by canon. That's in there from the beginning. What about Teachers? Well now you've got boys doing the teaching, and if you look carefully...

GT interrupts: Yeah the Teachers are supposed to watch over the church.

Greg: Yes, and the 14-year old, nah. So what do we wind up doing? Well we have them as junior companions and we'll have them prepare the sacrament. Where is that in scripture? It's not there. It's ok, but it's not there.

The Deacons are appendages anyway, so what do we do with them? Um, ok we'll have them pass the sacrament. I've got a copy of a letter written by President Grant to somebody who says, hey look. We've got this non-Mormon kid. He's very faithful. I presume he was not in church membership because at that time it required the consent of the parents for a boy to be baptized. But he comes out to meetings regularly. He's part of the Deacons quorum. H's not a member. Would it be ok if he passed the Sacrament? Yeah it would be ok.

GT: Oh really? This is what year?

Greg: This was in the '30s.

GT: In the 1930s.

Greg: I'm pretty sure that Keeler book was called *Lesser Priesthood and Church Governance*, but in that book, he said, "Any priesthood holder, and he had ranked the hierarchy as we normally do: high priests, seventies, elders, and then priests, teachers, deacons can ordain somebody to an equivalent or lower office, including the Aaronic Priesthood. Now we have still allowed priests to ordain to the Aaronic Priesthood.

GT: I believe that's canonical, right, in section 20?

Greg: I'd have to go back and look.

GT: Yeah Priests can ordain other priests. I'm pretty sure that's in there.[37]

Greg: The church for several decades were: a teacher can ordain a teacher or deacon; a deacon can ordain a deacon. One of the weirdest things that happened when I was doing my seven year research on priesthood, I was flying out to Los Angeles because I was lecturing at UCLA. It was shortly after laptop computers came out. I was doing data entry on my laptop as I was flying. I had a small book that I was copying from, because at that point I had to type it all in. The guy across the aisle looked and he saw it was an LDS book. He said, "You're LDS?"

"Yeah.

"I'm LDS too."

I said, "This is really fascinating in here because it says a deacon can ordain another deacon."

He said, "It's funny you mention that because I was ordained to the office of deacon by a deacon."

I said, "You've got to be kidding me."

He said, "No, I'll send you a photocopy of my ordination certificate," which he did.

GT: No Way.

---

[37] D&C 20:44-46 reads, "46 The priest's duty is to preach, teach, expound, exhort, and baptize, and administer the sacrament,
47 And visit the house of each member, and exhort them to pray vocally and in secret and attend to all family duties.
48 And he may also ordain other priests, teachers, and deacons."

Greg: It was about 1950.

GT: Wow!

Greg: Yeah.

GT: That's really recent.

Greg: Yeah, it's fluid. Don't get hung up.

GT chuckles: I think that would be great. I does seem to me, my son is 14 years old, actually he just turned 15 and he is actually my home teaching partner. It does seem to me that the bishops today, as opposed to the bishops when I was 14, do try to give the Aaronic Priesthood a little bit more responsibility. I know in our ward, they sit up with the high priests, and the bishopric at the beginning of opening exercises and give announcements and that sort of thing. It seems like they try to include them in prayers more often in priesthood meetings and that sort of a thing much more so than when I [was 14.] It's surprising to me to hear that in the '50s a deacon was ordaining a deacon and now we're not doing that. Why do you think that is?

Greg: Because somebody at a high level decided, no we're not going to do that anymore. Often that's what it comes down to.

GT: Alright, I really appreciate you spending so much time here on Gospel Tangents. I know these always go on longer, but I could probably sit here for another 2 hours and talk to you. I might have to make another appointment next time you're in town. So once again Greg Prince, thank you so much for taking some time and talking with us.

Greg: You're welcome!

Epilogue

I hope you enjoyed of listening to Greg Prince, and I'd like to thank him for spending so much time talking with us. In our next conversation, I'd like to introduce Dr. David Conley Nelson. He has written a book on the Mormon Church in Nazi Germany. He's got some really interesting insights into this. Check out this insight.

David: But they still had much more oversight by the German secret police. In fact the Germans and the Prussian secret police were so effective that they knew when missionaries were dispatched from Salt Lake City in making their way to the east coast to catch a ship to come to Germany. They knew because they had a secret police network among immigrants in the United States.

Additional Resources:

Here are links to the blog so you can join the conversation, as well as videos of the interview.

104: When did we start Ordaining Young Men?
https://gospeltangents.com/2017/12/09/lds-start-ordaining-youth/%20%E2%80%8E

103: Naturalist Explanation for Word of Wisdom?
https://gospeltangents.com/2017/12/06/naturalistic-explanation-word-wisdom/

102: Early LDS Priesthood: Similar to Ancient Christianity?
https://gospeltangents.com/2017/12/03/early-lds-priesthood-similar-ancient-christianity/

101: Ailing Church Leaders: "Not Ideal Governance."
https://wp.me/p8l6gx-IG

100: The 4 LDS Leadership Vacuums – What Happened?
https://gospeltangents.com/2017/11/27/4-leadership-vacuums-happened/

094: "There is Nothing in LDS Theology that Justifies Whacking Infants" (POX)
https://gospeltangents.com/2017/11/10/nothing-lds-theology-justifies-whacking-infants/

093: Greg Prince on History of LDS Policy Toward Gays
https://gospeltangents.com/2017/11/08/greg-prince-on-history-of-lds-policy-toward-gays/

We'd also love to have you visit our Amazon Store on our website to see other books on other Mormon topics. Be sure to check out our blog as well at https://GospelTangents.com to find information about future guests and projects we are working on. We would also like to partner with artists and musicians to produce a documentary on this and other topics. Please email us at GospelTangents@gmail.com if you're interested.

Thank you for your generous support!

www.ingramcontent.com/pod-product-compliance
Lightning Source LLC
Chambersburg PA
CBHW051232250726
48655CB00006B/2733